Discover The Impact On The Brain

# The Neuroscience Behind Emotional Wounds

Harrison S. Mungal, Ph.D., PsyD

**The Neuroscience Behind Emotional Wounds**

Copyright © 2023 Harrison S. Mungal

All rights reserved. Neither this publication nor any part of this publication may be reproduced or transmitted in any form or by any means, electronic or mechanical, including photocopying, recording or any information storage and retrieval system, without permission in writing from the author.

Printed in Canada

Contact author via email:
hsmungal@hotmail.com
www.agetoage.ca,
www.harrisonmungal.com
Facebook: Harrison Mungal
Twitter: HarrisonandKathleen @HKrelationships,
AgetoAge @agetoagec
LinkedIn: Harrison Mungal, Ph.D., PsyD
YouTube: Harrison Mungal
Instagram Harrisonmungal
Phone: 905-533-1334

# ABOUT the AUTHOR

Harrison holds two doctorate degrees, one in Clinical Psychology and the other in Philosophy in Social Work. He has two master's degrees, a master's degree in Social Work and a master's degree in Counselling. And a Bachelor's degree in Theology. He specializes in mental health, addictions, marriage and relationships, parenting, and family.

Harrison is considered one of the leading cognitive therapist workshop presenters. He wears many hats in supporting individuals, couples, families, and corporations. He has been a public speaker to over forty-two nations as a keynote speaker at conferences, seminars, and public events, as well as a speaker on several Radio and Television programs. He has written over twenty-five books. He is appreciated for the depth of his knowledge, great humour and passion for relationships, parenting, mental health, addictions, and other related life struggles.

Harrison utilizes a creative scientific-based approach to deliver compelling presentations that have granted him an excellent reputation. He has received several awards and recognitions from local police, mayors, community leaders, managers and directors, and families. He provides training and consultations to various community partners, including psychiatrists, medical doctors, social workers, nurses, police officers, firefighters and senior management teams.

Harrison has been involved in cognitive research to support individuals with addictions, psychosis, anxiety, and depression. He spearheaded several research studies on various themes, including music therapy and schizophrenia, vaccinations for children under six years old, substance abuse and addiction in the food service industry, and Thought Developmental Practice (TDP). His research on TDP with outpatient provided diversion methods to support substance abuse and addictions, anxiety, and depression under the supervision of the chief of psychiatry, Dr. David Koczerginski.

Harrison has over twenty-one years of professional experience working with diverse populations, including seventeen years in mental health and more than ten years as a psychotherapist. These diverse populations include youth and adult offenders, communities impacted by Acquired Brain Injuries, refugees, war victims, and those needing crisis-based support in various settings, i.e., liaison with police, hospitals, community agencies, and inpatient mental health settings.

Harrison specializes in evidence-based therapies, including Cognitive Behavioural Therapy (CBT), Cognitive Processing Therapy (CPT), Dialectical Behavioural Therapy (DBT), Thought Developmental Practice (TDP), Acceptance and Commitment Therapy (ACT), Interpersonal therapy (IPT), Motivational Interviewing Techniques, Grounding Techniques, Integrative Eclectic Therapy, Humanistic Experiential Therapy, Interpersonal Therapy, Supportive Therapy, Exposure Therapy, Visual Therapy, Psychodynamic Therapy.

# The Neuroscience Behind Emotional Wounds

# CONTENTS

| | | |
|---|---|---|
| 1 | The Neuroscience Behind Emotional Wounds. | 9 |
| 2 | Emotional Wounds | 21 |
| 3 | Wash The Brain | 31 |
| 4 | Rewire The Brain | 41 |

# THE NEUROSCIENCE BEHIND **EMOTIONAL WOUNDS**

Ever wonder how the brain responds to negative and positive influences? Let's delve deeper into the science behind our minds that have been emotionally wounded from traumas and abuses. Let's explore the role of cognitive dissonance and confirmation bias in maintaining the brain being affected and impacted by our environment. Cognitive dissonance occurs when an individual's beliefs, attitudes, and behaviours are inconsistent or conflicting. In the case of abuse, emotional wounds affect a person's existing core beliefs, and initial values are replaced with new ones that align with the new ideology or agenda. Confirmation bias is a psychological mechanism that contributes to a negative mind. It is the tendency to seek out information confirming one's beliefs while ignoring or dismissing information contradicting them.

Abused individuals often seek information supporting their beliefs and ignore or reject information that challenges them. Those with a wounded emotional mind may believe that a specific group of people (culture, ethnicity, sex, age group, demographics) are evil because of a passed-down mentality or perhaps one bad experience with one bad person, resulting in cognitive dissonance. They may have triggers when they meet someone kind and friendly from that group. To resolve this dissonance, the brain may rationalize the person's behaviour as an exception or interpret their actions negatively to maintain the belief system. This, however, does lead to discomfort and psychological stress. By understanding the mechanisms behind wounded emotions, we can better equip ourselves to resist future traumas, vicarious traumas, and abuses that affect our mental health. We need to protect ourselves and our emotional minds.

Understanding the anatomy and functioning of the brain concerning thought processes and a negative mind is crucial. The brain is a complex and intricate organ that controls our thoughts, actions, and emotions. It is made up of several parts, each with its unique function. The brain operates through a complex network of neurons, or nerve cells, which communicate with each other through chemical and electrical signals. Neurons form networks and pathways that control specific functions, allowing the brain to process information and produce responses.

In the 1960s, the Triune Brain model was introduced by neuroscientist Paul D. MacLean. It was suggested that the brain could be divided into three main parts: the Reptilian brain, which houses our survival instincts and manages autonomic body processes like breathing, heart rate, thirst, and hunger. The mammalian brain contains the limbic system, which regulates attachment and reproduction and processes our emotions like joy and fear. (The limbic system is another critical part of the brain that plays a crucial role in our emotions and memory. It comprises several structures, including the amygdala, hippocampus, and hypothalamus.

The amygdala processes emotions like fear, anger, and pleasure, while the hippocampus plays a vital role in memory formation and retrieval. The hypothalamus controls our body's functions, like hunger, thirst, and temperature.) The third part of the brain is the Neomammalian brain, which is responsible for learning, sensory processing, decision-making, memory, and complex problem-solving.

How our brain processes and interprets information influences our thought processes and thinking. Positive or negative experiences can affect the brain's neural pathways, strengthening or weakening them over time. A positive experience can create new neural pathways, while a negative experience can reinforce existing pathways, leading to a particular thought pattern or mindset. Understanding how the brain processes and stores information is essential to develop strategies for reprogramming the brain and cultivating a positive attitude. We can reshape our neural pathways with the proper techniques and tools, allowing us to adopt a more positive and empowering mindset.

A mind that has been impacted by negative experiences in life, like traumas, abuses, and criticism, results in psychological and physiological manifestations. This is a sign from our bodies that our emotions have been wounded. Psychological mechanisms, including cognitive dissonance, confirmation bias, and social influence, play a crucial role in developing and maintaining a negative mind. The physiological mechanisms release stress hormones, and the amygdala activation reinforces a negative mind.

Social influence is a powerful psychological mechanism that can contribute to a wounded emotion. Group pressure, social isolation, the spoken word, and manipulation of others can influence the beliefs and behaviours of someone emotionally wounded. Someone who is emotionally wounded can be like a tomato. They are sweet and juicy on the inside but have thin skin. They can feel the negative connotations in everything spoken, and anything connected to their sensory nerve (sight, hearing, touching, smelling, and tasting) can exacerbate the hurt they are experiencing.

It is essential to address any challenges or issues

we encounter in the present to avoid reinforcing our usual way of thinking and to change the way we will handle our thought processes in the future. This will increase the window of tolerance as the nervous system will no longer be in a constant state of stress. A minor traumatic event will no longer have a sizeable lasting impact as it will become manageable due to an increase in our emotional well-being.

Physiologically, the brain's response to stress plays a significant role in developing an abused mind. The amygdala, the brain's fear center, is activated when the brain perceives a threat. The amygdala is a small almond-shaped structure in the brain responsible for processing emotions and detecting environmental threats. When we encounter a potential threat, the amygdala sends a signal to the hypothalamus, which activates the body's "fight or flight" response. This response triggers a surge of hormones such as adrenaline and cortisol, which increase heart rate, blood pressure, and respiration to prepare the body for action.

The amygdala can reinforce negative thought patterns and beliefs in trauma and abuse. When a person is exposed to negative stimuli repeatedly; through the news, books, movies, social media or other forms of persuasion, the amygdala may become hypersensitive to these stimuli, causing the person to perceive them as even more threatening than they are. This can lead to heightened fear and anxiety, making it more difficult for the person to think critically or objectively.

The amygdala also plays a role in processing positive stimuli, including rewards and social connections. When we experience something pleasurable or rewarding, such as a delicious meal or a compliment from a friend, the amygdala releases dopamine, a neurotransmitter associated with pleasure and reward. This can help reinforce positive behaviours and beliefs and contribute to developing a more positive mindset.

Stress due to the perception of a threat also affects the brain's prefrontal cortex; rational thought is inhibited, making it difficult for the person to think logically and objectively. The prefrontal cortex is located at the front of the brain and is responsible for executive functions such as decision-making, planning, impulse control, and personality development. When exposed to negative stimuli, the prefrontal cortex can help regulate our emotional responses and prevent us from becoming overwhelmed.

Unfortunately, in these negative instances, the prefrontal cortex works against us in unison with the hippocampus by slowing down the process of learning new information to control our fear. We may have difficulty overriding the instinctual flight, fight, and freeze response, and we may also have difficulty thinking logically rather than emotionally.

Furthermore, prolonged exposure to stress and

trauma can change the brain's structure and functioning. Chronic stress can cause the hippocampus to shrink, leading to memory and cognitive impairments. The hippocampus is involved in memory formation and can help to encode positive experiences and reinforce positive beliefs. The brain's learning center becomes small and less active when we experience traumas. This causes issues with memory and problem-solving. Some of us may find it difficult to distinguish between the present and the past, creating a state of hypervigilance. It can also cause the amygdala to become overactive, leading to anxiety, fear, and other negative emotions.

Neurotransmitters, hormones, and other biochemical factors are crucial in shaping the brain's response to negative and positive influences. The release of the hormone cortisol in response to stress can profoundly impact brain function, impairing cognitive performance and reducing the ability to regulate emotions. Similarly, neurotransmitters like dopamine, serotonin, and norepinephrine regulate mood, motivation, and attention. Imbalances in these chemicals can contribute to the development of mental health disorders.

Wounded emotions, a by-product of trauma, can disrupt the balance of neurotransmitters and hormones in the brain, leading to long-term changes in brain function and behaviour. Individuals who have experienced trauma or chronic stress may have lower serotonin levels, contributing to symptoms of depression, anxiety, and other mental health problems.

Positive experiences and interventions like therapy, exercise, and meditation can help to restore balance to the brain's biochemical systems, promoting better mental health and resilience. Regular physical activity has been shown to increase neurotransmitters like dopamine and serotonin levels, improving mood and reducing the risk of depression.

Understanding the role of neurotransmitters, hormones, and other biochemical factors in brain function can be a vital step in overcoming wounds in our emotions by cultivating a positive mind. Individuals can take proactive steps towards better mental health and resilience in the face of negative influences by focusing on interventions that support a healthy biochemical balance in the brain.

One significant factor in the brain's response to positive influences is the release of neurotransmitters and hormones that promote pleasure, happiness, and well-being. These include dopamine, serotonin, oxytocin, and endorphins, among others. When we engage in activities like spending time with loved ones, listening to music, or pursuing our hobbies, the brain releases these feel-good chemicals, reinforcing our positive experiences and promoting a positive outlook.

The other important factor in the brain's response to positive influences is the process of neuroplasticity, which refers to the brain's ability to change and adapt over time in response to new experiences and stimuli. By engaging in activities that promote neuroplasticity, such as learning a new skill, practicing mindfulness, or engaging in creative endeavours, we can actively shape the structure and function of our brains to promote positive thought patterns and behaviours.

We need to recognize the role of social and environmental factors in shaping our mindset and outlook on life. Surrounding ourselves with positive and supportive individuals and engaging in activities that promote community and social connection can profoundly impact our physical and mental health and well-being. Positive interactions can bring healing to an emotional mind. Additionally, exposure to positive role models and inspirational stories can help to shift our perspective and inspire us to cultivate a more positive mindset.

One powerful technique for cultivating a positive mind is the practice of gratitude. By intentionally focusing on the things in our lives that we are grateful for, we can shift our perspective away from negative thoughts and feelings and towards a more optimistic outlook. This can be done through daily journaling, meditation, or simply taking time to reflect on the good things in our lives each day.

As we explore the intricacies of a wounded emotion, addressing the ethical implications of using evidence-based techniques is crucial. We can recondition our minds and restructure what we think to bring proper healing. We must know our triggers and work on diversion methods, grounding techniques, cognitive behavioural therapy, cognitive processing therapy and other evidence-based therapies. We must take care of our emotional being by protecting our minds from abuse and traumas.

Wounded emotions can have significant and long-lasting effects on an individual's mind and behaviour. While various factors can contribute to an abused mind, it is essential to recognize its impact on our lives, relationships, and work ethics. This can create a vulnerable environment for individuals who have been emotionally wounded.

Developing strategies to discern negative influences can reduce our vulnerability when our emotions are wounded. We must challenge harmful thoughts from ourselves and others that contribute to developing an abusive mind. Promoting values such as critical thinking, empathy, and individualism can create a more inclusive and resilient mind that is less vulnerable to the cause of our emotions being wounded.

Understanding cognitive dissonance is critical in breaking free from emotional wounds. By recognizing the discomfort and tension that arise when beliefs conflict with reality, individuals can begin to challenge and re-evaluate their beliefs. This can be a difficult and uncomfortable process, but it is essential in breaking free from the grip of the cause of being emotionally wounded.

In addition to recognizing cognitive dissonance, various strategies can be employed to overcome it. These include seeking out new information and experiences that challenge existing beliefs, practicing self-reflection and introspection, and seeking the support of trusted friends or professionals. Ultimately, overcoming cognitive dissonance requires a willingness to question deeply held beliefs and face uncomfortable truths, but the reward is an invaluable sense of freedom and autonomy.

# The Neuroscience Behind Emotional Wounds

# EMOTIONAL WOUNDS

Emotional wounds refer to psychological injuries that result from negative experiences such as trauma, rejection, loss, or abuse. They can affect our emotions, thoughts, and behaviour and be long-lasting if left unaddressed. These wounds are often hidden from others and may be hard to recognize or admit to ourselves. Emotional wounds can manifest in a variety of ways. They can cause us to feel anxious, depressed, angry, or hopeless. They can also lead to self-destructive behaviours such as substance abuse, overeating, or self-harm. Emotional wounds can be triggered by events or situations that remind us of the original trauma, leading to a cascade of negative emotions and thoughts.

Lily was a young woman who had grown up in a dysfunctional family. Her parents had a lot of issues, and they frequently fought, leaving Lily feeling anxious and insecure. As a result, she developed a deep fear of abandonment and struggled with trust issues in her relationships. One day, Lily fell in love with a man named Alex, and they started dating. However, Alex had a busy job and often had to work late, which triggered Lily's fear of abandonment. She would worry that he was cheating on her or that he didn't love her, even though he reassured her that he did.

As time went on, Lily's insecurities started to impact their relationship. She would become jealous and possessive, accusing Jake of things he hadn't done. Eventually, Alex couldn't take it anymore and ended the relationship, leaving Lily feeling devastated and alone. Even though Lily tried to move on, the emotional wounds from her childhood and the breakup with Jake continued to impact her. She struggled with depression and anxiety and had trouble trusting anyone else. It wasn't until Lily sought a therapist's help that she could heal her emotional wounds. Through therapy, she understood how her past experiences had shaped her behaviour and beliefs and learned new coping mechanisms to manage her anxiety and insecurity.

With time, Lily started to feel more confident and trust herself and others again. She even started dating someone new, and although it wasn't always easy, she was able to build a healthy relationship based on trust and mutual respect. Through her healing journey, Lily learned that emotional wounds could significantly impact our lives but that it is possible to move forward and live a fulfilling life with the proper support and self-care. So, if you are facing a similar situation, remember you are not alone on this journey, and with support and love, everything will be alright in the end – just trust the process!

Lily's story clearly shows that emotional wounds can significantly impact our mental health and brain function. They can affect our thoughts, emotions, and behaviour and lead to various mental health issues, such as anxiety, depression, post-traumatic stress disorder (PTSD), and addiction. Above all, emotional wounds can affect our ability to form healthy relationships. If we have experienced rejection or abandonment, we may have difficulty trusting others and creating close connections. This can lead to feelings of isolation and loneliness, further exacerbating mental health issues. These wounds even lead to changes in brain function and structure. Studies have shown that prolonged stress, such as that caused by trauma, can result in changes in the brain's system, process, and chemistry. This can lead to various issues, such as difficulty regulating emotions, memory problems, and difficulty concentrating.

Emotional wounds can also impact our physical health. Chronic stress and emotional distress have been linked to various physical health problems, such as heart disease, high blood pressure, and immune system dysfunction. This is because prolonged stress can lead to inflammation in the body, which can contribute to the developing of these health issues. Therefore, it is imperative to address emotional wounds and seek support to prevent them from negatively impacting our mental and physical health. Therapy, support groups, and self-care practices such as meditation and exercise can help heal emotional wounds and promote overall well-being.

Emotional wounds are hidden impacts on our minds that are difficult to recognize and can be caused by several reasons. Trauma is one of the most common causes of emotional wounds that could result from events such as physical or sexual abuse, neglect, violence, natural disasters, or accidents. These experiences can leave us feeling overwhelmed, helpless, and unable to cope with the world around us. Like trauma that went long-lasting drastic effects on our minds, rejection is another common factor contributing to mental wounds. Being rejected by someone we love, whether a romantic partner, family member, or friend, can leave us feeling unwanted, unloved, and worthless. The rejection can come as a breakup, a fight, or simply feeling left out. Whatever the cause, rejection can leave a deep emotional wound that can be hard to heal.

This list of causes also includes 'Loss' and 'Abuse' as top culprits behind emotional wounding. Losing someone we love, whether due to death or separation, can leave us feeling alone, empty, and hopeless. Grief can take many forms and can last for months or even years. Similarly, abuse, another cause of emotional wounds, come in many forms, including physical, sexual, verbal, or emotional. Emotional abuse can be particularly insidious as it is often hidden and may not leave visible scars. It involves tactics such as gaslighting, manipulation, or constantly putting someone down. This can lead to feelings of low self-esteem, worthlessness, and anxiety. It's essential to allow ourselves to grieve and process our emotions during this time to avoid prolonged emotional wounds.

We should understand that these emotional wounds do not always result from a single traumatic event. They can also result from ongoing stress, chronic illness, or difficult life circumstances. For example, living in poverty, dealing with a chronic illness, or experiencing discrimination can all lead to emotional wounds over time. But whatever the actual reason, emotional wounds can significantly impact our lives. They can affect our relationships, our ability to trust others, and our overall sense of well-being. They can also lead to physical symptoms such as headaches, stomach aches, or chronic pain. If left unaddressed, emotional wounds can continue impacting our lives for years. However, there are steps we can take to heal from emotional wounds. Seeking therapy, talking to a trusted friend or family member, practicing self-care, and engaging in activities that bring us joy can all help us to heal and move forward.

As we know, emotional pain can manifest in various physical and mental ways, affecting our mood, behaviour, and even physical health. For example, if we experience a traumatic event such as a car accident or losing a loved one, we may feel anxious or depressed.

We may struggle to focus at work or have trouble sleeping at night. We may also feel more irritable or short-tempered than usual, impacting our relationships with others. There would be a toll on our self-esteem and sense of self-worth too. If we experience rejection or criticism from someone we care about, it can leave us feeling inadequate or unworthy. This can lead to negative self-talk or a tendency to self-sabotage in our personal and professional lives.

The worst emotional wounds can do to us is the development of avoidance or numbing behaviours. If we experience something traumatic or painful, we may try to avoid anything that reminds us of the experience. For example, in a car accident, we may avoid driving or riding in a car. If we experience a loss, we may avoid certain places or activities that we associate with the person we lost. This can lead to social isolation and a loss of enjoyment in things we used to find pleasurable. However, despite the negative impact that emotional wounds can have on our everyday life, it's important to remember that healing is possible. There are many ways to bring healing, like engaging in self-care activities such as exercise, mindfulness, or spending time in nature to reduce damage and promote emotional well-being.

The crux of all emotional wounds is the encounter with the traumatic event or a series of emotionally distressing events. For example, a person physically abused as a child may carry emotional wounds well into adulthood. These wounds can impact how the person thinks, feels, and behaves daily. Moreover, their mind may become filled with negative thoughts and emotions. They may experience feelings of sadness, anger, or shame that they can't seem to shake. Their mind may feel cluttered and overwhelmed, making it difficult to focus on everyday tasks or activities they once enjoyed.

In the majority of cases, emotional wounds represent themselves in the form of anxiety, depression, or other mental health issues; for example, someone who was bullied in school may develop social anxiety as a result of their experiences. When it comes to emotional wounds, it's essential to understand that the severity of the wound doesn't necessarily correlate with the time it takes to heal. Just like a rug burn may be a minor physical wound that recovers quickly, some emotional wounds may be relatively minor and heal quickly, while others may be more severe and take much longer to heal.

For example, let's say you had a minor argument with a friend that resulted in hurt feelings. This may be considered a minor emotional wound, similar to a rug burn. While it may cause some discomfort or pain at the moment, with some time and communication, the wound can heal relatively quickly. You and your friend may talk it out, apologize, and move on from the argument, leaving the emotional wound in the past.

On the other hand, a more severe emotional wound, such as experiencing childhood trauma or abuse, may be more akin to a deep cut. These emotional wounds can be very deep and impactful and may require more time and effort to heal. In some cases, the wound may never fully recover, but with the proper treatment and support, individuals can learn to manage their emotions and live fulfilling lives.

It's important to note that the healing process for emotional wounds is not always linear. Like how a physical wound may appear healing but suddenly become inflamed or infected, emotional wounds can sometimes resurface unexpectedly. Triggers such as anniversaries of the traumatic event, encountering the person who caused the emotional wound, or even certain smells or sounds can bring back painful emotions and memories.

To heal from emotional wounds, it's important to acknowledge their existence and seek support from a mental health professional if needed. Just like you may need to clean and dress a physical wound to prevent infection, seeking professional help can give you the tools and support you need to heal emotionally. This may include therapy, medication, or other forms of treatment, depending on the severity of the wound and the individual's unique needs. In addition to seeking professional help, individuals can do things independently to help facilitate the healing process.

These may include engaging in self-care activities such as exercise, mindfulness practices, journaling, or spending time in nature. A support system of friends and family who can offer empathy, understanding, and validation is also essential.

Ultimately, healing from emotional wounds is a journey, and it's crucial to approach it with a sense of curiosity and openness. By acknowledging and addressing emotional wounds, individuals can learn to live more fully in the present moment and move forward with a greater sense of resilience and self-awareness. Emotional wounds can impact each person differently, and there's no right or wrong way to feel after experiencing trauma or distressing events. However, if the wounds are left unaddressed, they can lead to a messed up brain and make it difficult for the person to move forward in their life.

# Wash
## The Brain

Traumatic experiences, abusive situations, and mental illnesses can make a person vulnerable to manipulation and control. We can become susceptible to manipulation when affected by negative experiences in life.

Trauma can be a powerful tool to break down an individual's sense of self and instill new beliefs or values. Trauma can come in many forms, such as physical, emotional, or sexual abuse, natural disasters, accidents, and violent crimes. The effects of trauma can be long-lasting and deeply ingrained, making it an effective method for those seeking to manipulate and control others.

Abusive relationships are, unfortunately, far too common in our world today. Whether it's physical, emotional, or verbal abuse can have devastating effects on the victim's mental and emotional well-being. It can be challenging to understand why someone would stay in such a toxic situation, but the reality is that abusive relationships can be complicated to break free from.

One of the reasons why abusive relationships can be so difficult to leave is that the abuser often manipulates the victim's thoughts and emotions. They use various tactics to control their partner, such as gaslighting, guilt-tripping, and isolating them from friends and family. Over time, the victim's sense of reality can become distorted, and they may begin to believe that they deserve the abuse or that it's their fault. This is why we need to "wash the brain" of those who have been in abusive relationships.

By "Washing the brain" does not mean erasing memories or negative manipulation someone to think a certain way. Instead, it means helping the victim to regain control over their thoughts and emotions. When someone has been in an abusive relationship for a long time, it can be challenging to separate their beliefs and feelings from those imposed on them by their abuser. This is where therapy and other forms of support can be beneficial.

Consider the story of Sarah and Jack. Sarah had been with Jack for several years, and while the relationship had started well, it gradually became abusive. Jack would often belittle Sarah, call her names, and make her feel like she was never good enough. He would also control her finances and forbid her from seeing her friends and family.

At first, Sarah tried to resist Jack's control, but over time, she began to internalize his criticisms and doubt her abilities. She felt she couldn't make decisions without his approval and was nothing without him.

This is a classic example of how abusive relationships can lead to manipulation. Jack could gain complete control over her thoughts and actions by systematically breaking Sarah's self-esteem and isolating her from her support network. Sarah had been brainwashed into believing she was nothing without Jack and that he was the only one who could make her happy.

Unfortunately, Sarah's story is not unique. Many people find themselves in abusive relationships where they are brainwashed into believing that their partner's abusive behaviour is normal or even justified. It's essential to recognize the signs of abuse and seek help if you or someone you know is in an abusive relationship. With the proper support and resources, it's possible to break free from the cycle of abuse and overcome the effects of manipulation.

Individuals who suffer from mental illnesses such as depression and anxiety are often more vulnerable to manipulation and negative manipulation tactics. These conditions can impact a person's sense of self-worth, decision-making abilities, and ability to analyze information critically. As a result, those who struggle with mental illness may be more susceptible to the influence of others.

For example, someone with depression may feel hopeless and powerless, leading them to seek guidance and direction from others. If they come across someone who appears confident and knowledgeable, they may be more likely to trust that person and be swayed by their ideas and opinions.

Similarly, someone with anxiety may struggle with decision-making and may be more likely to rely on others to choose. This can make them more susceptible to the influence of someone who presents as a strong and decisive leader.

In addition, mentally ill individuals may be more easily manipulated through gaslighting tactics, making them doubt their perceptions and reality. This can further erode their sense of self and make them more susceptible to the influence of a manipulator.

It's important to note that mental illness is not a weakness or a flaw, and individuals with it are not inherently more susceptible to manipulation. However, it's important to recognize that certain conditions can make individuals more vulnerable to manipulation and to seek help and support when needed.

Here are two case studies of individuals manipulated through traumatic experiences or abusive relationships. Jane was a survivour of childhood sexual abuse. As an adult, she joined a religious cult that promised her healing and redemption. The cult leader exploited Jane's vulnerability and trauma history to control and manipulated her. Over time, Jane became increasingly isolated from her family and friends as the cult demanded more and more of her time and resources. The cult leader convinced Jane that he was the only one who truly understood her pain and that the group was the only place where she could find acceptance and love. It took years of therapy for Jane to break free from the cult's grip and heal from her trauma.

Tom was in a long-term relationship with his partner, who was emotionally and physically abusive. Over time, his partner became increasingly controlling and manipulative, using tactics such as gaslighting and isolation to maintain power and control over Tom. Tom's partner convinced him he was worthless and unlovable without them and that no one else would ever want him. Tom began to believe these lies and became increasingly dependent on his partner for validation and emotional support. It wasn't until Tom sought therapy and began to build a support system outside of the abusive relationship that he could see the truth and break free from the manipulation.

These examples demonstrate how individuals can be susceptible to manipulation through traumatic experiences or abusive relationships. It's essential to seek help and support if you or someone you know is in a similar situation.

When an individual has experienced trauma or abuse, the effects of manipulation can be particularly insidious and long-lasting. In some cases, the manipulation results may persist for years, or even decades, after the initial traumatic event.

One potential long-term effect of manipulation is the development of Post-Traumatic Stress Disorder (PTSD). This condition can cause individuals to experience symptoms such as flashbacks, nightmares, intrusive thoughts, hypervigilance, and intense anxiety or panic. These symptoms can make it difficult for individuals to function daily and significantly impact their relationships, work, and overall well-being.

Another potential long-term effect of manipulation is developing a deep mistrust in others. When an individual has been subjected to manipulation, they may struggle to trust others, particularly authority figures or those in positions of power. This can lead to feelings of isolation and loneliness and difficulty forming and maintaining meaningful relationships.

In addition, negative manipulation can also impact an individual's sense of identity. When an individual has been manipulated, they may have difficulty separating their beliefs and values from those imposed upon them. This can lead to confusion, a lack of direction in life, and feelings of guilt or shame for not being able to live up to the expectations of others.

It is important to note that not all individuals who have experienced trauma or abuse will develop long-term effects of manipulation. However, for those who do, the impact can be significant and may require ongoing support and treatment to address.

Abusers use a variety of techniques to brainwash their victims, and these techniques are often very effective. One method commonly used in isolation is where the abuser or manipulator cuts off their victim from friends and family, leaving them with nobody to turn to for help or support. This can create a dependency on the abuser or manipulator, making it difficult for the victim to leave.

Another technique is gaslighting, where the abuser or manipulator makes the victim doubt their thoughts, feelings, and perceptions. This can create confusion and disorientation, causing the victim more vulnerable to manipulation. The abuser or manipulator may also use physical or emotional abuse to control the victim, reinforcing the sense of helplessness and dependency.

In some cases, the abuser or manipulator may use tactics such as love bombing, where they shower the victim with affection and attention to create a sense of loyalty and dependence. They may also use coercion or threats to control the victim's behaviour, such as threatening to harm themselves or others if the victim doesn't comply with their demands.

It's important to be aware of these techniques and to seek help if you or someone you know is experiencing abuse or manipulation. With support and resources, it is possible to break free from the effects of manipulation and regain control of one's life.

When someone has experienced trauma or abuse or is struggling with a mental illness, they can be more susceptible to manipulation. Therefore, it is vital to recognize the signs of manipulation to help those working. Some common symptoms of manipulation include a loss of personal identity, sudden changes in behaviour or beliefs, extreme fear and anxiety, and dependence on a specific person or group. It's essential to pay attention to changes in behaviour and personality and to trust your instincts if you suspect someone may be experiencing manipulation.

Recognizing the signs of negative manipulation can also help prevent individuals from being further manipulated or abused. By intervening early on and providing support and resources, it may be possible to prevent the individual from experiencing further harm. It's essential to approach the situation with empathy and understanding while setting clear boundaries and advocating for the individual's safety and well-being.

Additionally, healthcare professionals, therapists, and other support systems must be trained to identify and treat individuals who have experienced manipulation. This can involve trauma-informed care, which considers the unique experiences and needs of individuals who have experienced trauma or abuse. By recognizing the signs of manipulation and providing appropriate support, we can help those who have experienced trauma, misuse, or mental illness reclaim their identity and autonomy.

In conclusion to this chapter, it's essential to recognize the potential long-term effects of negative manipulation or manipulation in individuals who have experienced trauma, abuse, or mental illness. By understanding the techniques used by abusers and manipulators to manipulate their victims, we can better equip ourselves with the knowledge and tools needed to identify and intervene in such situations. Providing trauma-informed care to those who have experienced manipulation through trauma, abuse, or mental illness is crucial.

Moving forward, the next chapter will focus on a standard tool used in manipulation: relationship issues. We will examine how manipulators use relationship dynamics to control and manipulate their victims. By understanding the tactics used in these situations, we can work towards building healthier relationships and avoid falling victim to such manipulation tactics.

# Rewire
## The Brain

When it comes to treating mental health issues, many approaches can be practical. One of the most widely used and researched methods is cognitive behavioural therapy (CBT). CBT is a type of talk therapy that is highly effective in treating various mental health issues, including anxiety disorders, depression, trauma, PTSD, OCD, and addiction. Restructuring our thoughts and beliefs can change how we feel and behave, leading to greater happiness and fulfillment. In this chapter, we will explore the principles of CBT and how it can be used to recondition our minds and overcome negative thought patterns.

One significant benefit of CBT is that it provides individuals with tools to recognize and manage their triggers. The goal of CBT is not to eliminate stress and anxiety but to provide individuals with the tools to manage them effectively. With CBT, individuals learn to identify triggers and develop strategies to address them proactively. This can include deep breathing, progressive muscle relaxation, and mindfulness meditation.

Another benefit of CBT is that it is focused on the present and future rather than dwelling on past events. This approach helps individuals break the cycle of negative thoughts and behaviours, which can be deeply ingrained in their lives. CBT sessions are typically goal-oriented, with therapists and individuals working together to develop a specific plan for managing stress and anxiety.

CBT is also highly customizable to individual needs, effectively treating various mental health issues. If someone is struggling with depression, CBT can help that individual to identify and challenge negative thought patterns such as, "I'm worthless" or "Nothing will ever get better." By replacing these thoughts with more positive and realistic ones, individuals can feel better and engage in positive behaviours such as self-care and socializing. In treating addiction, individuals identify and challenge negative thoughts and behaviours that may be contributing to their substance use. Individuals can reduce their reliance on substances and improve their overall mental health by positively coping with stress and negative emotions. CBT sessions may include role-playing exercises, cognitive restructuring, and behavioural experiments to help individuals learn and practice new coping strategies.

Furthermore, CBT is a relatively short-term therapy, with individuals often seeing significant results within just a few weeks. This can be highly beneficial for individuals dealing with acute mental health issues and needing quick relief. CBT is also cost-effective compared to other forms of therapy, making it more accessible to individuals who may not have access to extensive mental health care.

As we delve deeper into the power of Cognitive Behavioural Therapy (CBT), it becomes increasingly clear that this therapy can be an effective tool for building resilience and improving self-esteem. Working with a trained therapist, individuals can learn to restructure their thoughts and beliefs to support their mental health and well-being.

Through CBT, clients learn to recognize and challenge negative thought patterns and beliefs contributing to anxiety, depression, and other mental health issues. By identifying these patterns and learning to reframe them in a more positive light, individuals can build a more positive self-image and cultivate a sense of self-worth.

CBT also teaches clients coping skills for managing stress and anxiety daily. By learning to identify triggers and develop effective coping strategies, individuals can feel more in control of their emotions and better equipped to handle the challenges that life throws their way.

Another critical aspect of CBT is its focus on goal-setting and problem-solving. By working with a therapist to identify specific goals and develop actionable steps for achieving them, individuals can build a sense of purpose and direction in their lives. This can be especially helpful for those struggling with addiction, as it provides a roadmap for recovery and helps to build motivation and momentum toward long-term sobriety.

Let us now understand the relationship between thoughts, emotions, and behaviours. CBT operates on the principle that our thoughts influence our feelings, and our emotions then influence our behaviours. This cycle can be positive or negative, depending on our thoughts. For example, if we have negative thoughts about a situation, we may feel anxious or depressed, leading to negative coping behaviours such as avoidance or isolation. On the other hand, if we have positive thoughts, we may feel happy and confident, leading to behaviours that reinforce those emotions.

CBT works to identify negative thoughts and replace them with more positive, realistic ones. This is done by examining the evidence for and against a particular thought and then developing a more balanced perspective. For example, if someone thinks, "I'm a failure because I didn't get the promotion," a CBT therapist may ask them to examine the evidence for and against this thought. They may find that while they didn't get the promotion, they have received positive feedback from their boss in the past and have made significant contributions to the company. This process can help to restructure their thoughts and improve their emotional and behavioural responses.

One of the critical components of CBT is

identifying and challenging cognitive distortions. These are patterns of thinking that are inaccurate, irrational, or unhelpful. Some common cognitive distortions include all-or-nothing review (seeing things in black-and-white terms), jumping to conclusions (assuming the worst without evidence), and overgeneralization (making sweeping statements based on limited evidence). Individuals can learn to think more realistically and positively by identifying and challenging these distortions, improving emotional and behavioural outcomes.

The first step in addressing negative thought patterns is to identify them. This can be done by paying attention to our internal dialogue and recognizing when we engage in self-defeating thoughts. For example, if we're feeling anxious about an upcoming job interview and thinking, "I'm never going to get this job," that's an example of black-and-white thinking. It's important to recognize when we're engaging in these types of thought patterns so that we can begin to challenge them.

Once we've identified negative thought patterns, the next step is to challenge them using evidence-based techniques. This might involve asking ourselves, "Is this thought true?" or "What evidence do I have to support this thought?" Challenging negative thoughts can restructure our thinking more positively and realistically.

Another technique used in CBT for challenging negative thought patterns is called "decatastrophizing."

This involves breaking down a catastrophic thought into smaller, more manageable pieces. For example, if we're thinking, "If I fail this test, my life is over," we might challenge that thought by asking ourselves, "Is it true that my life will be over? What would be the worst thing that could happen?" This technique can help us put our thoughts into perspective and avoid catastrophizing.

CBT also involves teaching clients coping strategies for managing negative thoughts when they arise. One common technique, "thought-stopping," consists of recognizing negative thoughts and replacing them with more positive or neutral ones. This can be done by saying "stop" to ourselves when we notice negative thoughts and then immediately replacing them with a more positive or neutral thought.

Understanding the role of automatic thoughts and core beliefs in this process is essential. Our automatic thoughts are the immediate and spontaneous thoughts that pop into our heads in response to a situation or event. These thoughts can be positive, negative, or neutral, influencing our mood and behaviour. We learn to recognize and examine these automatic thoughts in CBT for accuracy and usefulness.

On the other hand, core beliefs are deeply ingrained beliefs about ourselves, others, and the world around us. These beliefs often develop early in life and can be influenced by our experiences, upbringing, culture, and values. Core beliefs can be either positive or negative and can significantly impact our self-esteem, self-worth, and overall mental health.

In CBT, we learn to identify and challenge our negative core beliefs, replacing them with more positive and realistic ones. Doing so can change how we think, feel, and behave, leading to a more positive and fulfilling life. For example, if someone has a negative core belief that they are unlovable, they may have automatic thoughts such as, "No one will ever love me," or, "I'm not good enough for a relationship." Through CBT, they can challenge these thoughts and replace them with more positive and accurate ones, such as, "I am worthy of love" or, "I have many positive qualities that make me a great partner."

Goal-setting plays a critical role in the success of this therapeutic approach. Setting achievable goals in CBT cannot be overstated, as it serves as the foundation for progress. At the outset of treatment, it is essential to establish a clear understanding of what the client wants to achieve. The therapist and client can then work together to develop a plan for achieving those goals, which includes breaking them down into smaller, more manageable steps.

One of the key benefits of setting achievable goals in CBT is that it helps to provide a sense of direction and purpose. When a person struggles with mental health issues such as anxiety, depression, or addiction, they may feel lost and unsure how to move forward. By setting clear goals and developing a plan for achieving them, the client can gain control over their situation and begin to progress towards their desired outcome.

Another benefit of goal-setting in CBT is that it provides a way to measure progress. When people work towards a goal, they can track their progress. This can be incredibly motivating, as it allows them to see the tangible results of their efforts. It also helps to break down the overall task into smaller, more achievable steps, making the process less overwhelming.

However, it is essential to note that the goals set in CBT must be realistic and achievable. Setting too lofty or unrealistic goals can be counterproductive, as the client may become discouraged when they cannot achieve them. Therefore, it is essential to consider the client's needs and capabilities when setting goals, ensuring they are challenging yet attainable.

In addition to the benefits of goal-setting in CBT, it is also important to recognize that progress may not always be linear. There will be setbacks and obstacles, and preparing for these challenges is crucial. This is where the smaller, more achievable goals come in handy, as they provide a way to continue progressing even when faced with setbacks.

If you're interested in exploring cognitive behavioural therapy (CBT) to restructure your thoughts and manage mental health issues such as anxiety, depression or addiction, finding a qualified therapist is essential. You can start by asking your primary care physician or mental health provider for a referral to find a qualified CBT therapist. You can also search online for licensed therapists specializing in CBT. Read their credentials and experience to ensure they fit your needs well.

Once you have found a potential therapist, you must ask questions during your first session to ensure they match you well. Ask about their CBT experience, training, therapy approach, and what to expect during sessions. It's vital that you feel comfortable with your therapist and that you trust their expertise.

During CBT sessions, you can expect to work collaboratively with your therapist to identify negative or unhelpful thoughts and behaviours that may be contributing to your mental health issues. Your therapist will help you learn techniques to restructure these thoughts and behaviours into more positive and helpful patterns. They may assign homework between sessions to help you practice these techniques and track your progress.

It's important to remember that therapy is a process, and progress may not happen overnight. But with dedication and effort, CBT can help you restructure your thoughts and improve your mental health and overall well-being. By working with a qualified therapist and practicing CBT techniques, you can gain the tools and skills to control your thoughts and build a healthier life.

Nowadays, technology has played a significant role in its evolution. With the advent of smartphones and other digital devices, therapy has become more accessible. Online treatment and mobile apps have made it possible for people to receive CBT from the comfort of their own homes, making therapy more convenient and cost-effective.

Online therapy has become increasingly popular as people seek alternatives to traditional in-person therapy sessions. This form of treatment allows individuals to communicate with a licensed therapist through video or chat, allowing them to receive therapy on schedule. Online therapy treats various mental health conditions, including anxiety, depression, and post-traumatic stress disorder.

Mobile apps have also become famous for people looking to incorporate CBT into their daily lives. These apps offer a range of features, including mood tracking, guided meditations, and journaling prompts. They also provide users access to cognitive restructuring exercises and coping strategies for anxiety and depression. Some apps even incorporate gamification elements, turning therapy into a fun and engaging experience.

One of the key advantages of using technology in CBT is that it allows for a more personalized approach to therapy. With online therapy and mobile apps, individuals can receive treatment tailored to their needs and preferences. For example, a person who struggles with social anxiety may benefit from an app that includes exposure therapy exercises. Someone dealing with depression may find that mood tracking and positive affirmations are more helpful.

Another advantage of using technology in CBT is that it removes many barriers preventing people from seeking therapy. For example, people who live in rural or remote areas may have limited access to mental health services. Online treatment and mobile apps allow these individuals to receive therapy without travelling long distances or taking time off work. Similarly, people who are hesitant to seek therapy due to the stigma associated with mental illness may feel more comfortable using a mobile app or participating in online therapy sessions.

However, it's important to note that while technology can be a valuable tool in CBT, it's not a substitute for in-person therapy when needed. Online treatment and mobile apps may not be suitable for everyone, and individuals should work with their healthcare provider to determine the best course of treatment for their specific needs.

As discussed throughout this chapter, Cognitive Behavioural Therapy (CBT) can be incredibly effective for restructuring your thoughts and overcoming mental health challenges such as anxiety, depression, trauma, and addiction. However, it's important to remember that progress doesn't happen overnight, and maintaining your progress is critical to long-term success.

A critical aspect of maintaining progress is to continue practicing the skills and techniques you've learned in CBT, even after your sessions have ended. This may mean continuing to challenge negative thought patterns, practicing relaxation and mindfulness techniques, or actively working on changing unhealthy behaviours. Setting goals for yourself and creating a plan to continue working on your mental health outside therapy can be helpful.

It's also important to recognize that setbacks may occur, and that's okay. It's natural to experience ups and downs as you work on reconditioning your mind and building new thought patterns. Don't let setbacks discourage you or cause you to give up on the progress you've made. Instead, use them as an opportunity to learn and grow and to further hone your skills in managing your thoughts and emotions.

Another critical aspect of maintaining progress is to continue seeking support as needed. This may mean scheduling occasional follow-up sessions with your CBT therapist or seeking other forms of support, such as group therapy or a support group. Additionally, it's essential to communicate openly with loved ones about your mental health journey and ask for their support as needed.

Ultimately, it is essential to remember that mental health is an ongoing journey and that there is no "quick fix" for overcoming challenges such as anxiety or depression. However, you can restructure your thoughts and build a more positive, fulfilling life with commitment, persistence, and the right tools and support. CBT is just one of many tools available to help you on this journey, and by practicing the techniques and strategies you've learned, you can continue to progress and achieve your mental health goals.

When restructuring our thoughts, Cognitive Behavioural Therapy (CBT) offers a variety of effective strategies. Here are ten fundamental techniques that can help you replace negative beliefs with positive ones:

**1. Identify negative self-talk:** The first step in restructuring your thoughts is to identify negative self-talk. Notice the critical and judgmental voice in your head and recognize when it starts to emerge.

**2. Challenge negative thoughts:** Once you've identified negative self-talk, you can challenge it. Ask yourself if the thought is accurate and if there's any evidence to support it.

**3. Reframe negative thoughts:** Instead of dwelling on negative thoughts, try reframing them positively. For example, instead of thinking, "I can't do this," reframe it to, "I haven't done this before, but I can learn how to do it."

**4. Practice positive affirmations:** Use positive affirmations to rewire your brain with positive beliefs. Repeat affirmations like "I am capable and worthy" and

"I am strong and resilient" regularly.

**5. Use visualization:** Visualize positive outcomes to help restructure your thoughts. Imagine succeeding at a task or achieving a goal to reinforce positive beliefs.

**6. Take action:** Take action towards your goals, even if it's just a tiny step. Accomplishing even small tasks can help build positive beliefs and restructure negative ones.

**7. Practice gratitude:** Focus on the positive things in your life and cultivate a daily gratitude practice. This can help rewire your brain to focus on the good instead of the negative.

**8. Refocus your attention:** When negative thoughts start to take over, refocus on something positive. This could be a happy memory, a favourite song, or a calming activity like meditation.

**9. Use positive self-talk:** Replace negative self-talk with positive self-talk. Instead of saying, "I'm not good enough," say, "I am capable and competent."

**10. Seek support:** Finally, don't be afraid to seek permission from a therapist or mental health professional. They can help you restructure your thoughts and beliefs and provide additional strategies and tools to support your mental health.

# The Neuroscience Behind Emotional Wounds

# The Neuroscience Behind Emotional Wounds

# PROTECTIVE FACTORS

We must protect our minds, like our physical bodies, from fear. When the mind is scarred, it takes some of us a long time to accept. And in the process of healing, there are several psychological issues we need to come to terms with. We can avoid mental health traits from becoming a formal diagnosis of mental illness.

Taking care of our mental health can help reduce many unnecessary issues in life that can be prevented. We can preserve our ability to have a much more enjoyable life instead of using the negative impact as a "crutch" or excuse to live miserably and unhappily. We need to remember that happiness is a choice! Endless happiness and mental wellness are paramount to preventing long-lasting issues than cannot be reversed. Soul care is the tool we can use to prevent this from happening. Restoring our mental health is vital to living in peace and having a life full of happiness.

As we have seen, mental illness is actual. It can be measured by the symptoms experienced, just like a physical illness—mental health challenges the brain's functionality and how information is processed. We must take every caution possible to avoid the negative progression of one's mental health. If it is like a rug burn, let's prevent it from becoming a deep cut. Prevention is the key to staying healthy and preventing our mental health from formulating a diagnosis.

To prevent something from happening means to do something about it before it happens – think about eating healthy versus taking medicine for heartburn. One addresses the root cause, and the other has to work against the effect produced. Prevention is the root cause; it is effective in the formational stages, and to no surprise, it is the secret hidden in our daily habits.

We can do much better if we learn the power of psychological resiliency to balance our lives by choosing healthy activities and taking on responsibility. Our daily routine can be disrupted with stress, anxiety and depression, but we have an internal power to help us become 'overcomers' by taking the proper steps. Some practical ways to support our mental health include developing a routine with regular exercise, eating healthy foods, sleeping at least seven to eight hours a night, practicing deep breathing or meditation and forming an excellent social network where you can interact and avoid intrusive thoughts.

Journaling is another great practice of manipulating the brain to clean out the soul of unprocessed emotions by emptying your thoughts on paper, challenging your negative thoughts by putting them on trial, practicing positivity and optimism, and being grateful. A trend that has gained much popularity in recent years is the practice of keeping a so-called 'gratitude journal' where you just list things you are thankful for. This practice rewires the brain to be more positive and excited about life.

Look at it like risk factors versus protective factors. Contextual variables can help or hinder a child's development as they become competent individuals. Psychologists refer to them as risk and protective factors. You might already know about risk factors; however, protective factors are just as important.

The state of our mental health is influenced by the presence or absence of numerous protective and risk factors, including a diverse combination of these factors. Identifying protective and risk variables in children and adolescents can help guide prevention and intervention methods. If mental health illnesses are present, protective and risk factors may impact their course, especially when you have a family history of mental illness. We can also identify protective and risk factors on our journey to better care for our souls.

Some examples of such protective factors include physical growth and development, intellectual growth and academic success, coping abilities and problem-solving. Emotional self-control and a person's sense of self-worth are also vital. What is beneficial is being connected and engaged in healthy relationships with other people. Psychologists suggest that a person needs to be well-connected in two or more contexts:

community, school, sports, work, religion, and culture. This can also take the form of mentorship or talent-development coaches. For children to thrive, they also need relationships with supportive family members. This includes a sense of clear values, limitations, structure, predictability, and standards for behaviour.

Positive social norms are a significant contributor to physical and mental well-being. All of these are protective factors when intact, but they could be risk factors when not working as they should. For example, Predictability in family life helps a person to have a sense of normalcy and stability. Without that, they could feel like they must walk on eggshells or that a bomb could go off any second. It is impossible to feel safe with a highly unpredictable person. One of the characteristics of God that we have focused on is that He is the same yesterday, today, and tomorrow.

Disturbance of these factors all comes into play when developing mental disorders such as anxiety, depression, and addiction. Some may say they may not matter much when developing genetic mental illness disorders. However, these factors are essential for living a well-balanced life despite suffering from them.

A person with a mental illness would benefit even more by applying these factors than somebody doing 'well' mentally. If you or someone in your family has been treated for mental illness, it's also helpful to know which therapies have worked and which didn't.

Just keep in mind that you are still a unique individual. There is no replacement for choosing the treatment that is right for you. Knowing your family history might also help you in making better lifestyle selections. For example: If you have a family history of addiction, it's usually a good idea to be cautious about your drug and alcohol use. Or, if you have a family history of schizophrenia, it is helpful to know that there is quite a lot of evidence that marijuana usage can cause psychosis.

The good news is that genetic links to mental illness can help you understand your symptoms, get a faster diagnosis, and learn more about your family history. When you're still unsure about your diagnosis or worry that you're fooling yourself or making things up, the overwhelming evidence that certain conditions can be passed down might save you time.

You are not doomed, and you do not need to be afraid of opening the closet, scared of the skeletons that might fall out. Your role in your family is to be a blessing to all and to glorify God; one way of doing that is to teach your family how we can care for our souls. This might seem simple, but if you are the first person in your family to do this soul work, you break intergenerational cycles and rewrite the story for future generations. God wants to use you mightily in your family! Your first mission field is found around your dining table.

Getting your diagnosis may help you better appreciate a family member who was never officially diagnosed but had a mental disorder that you suspected. For example, you might grow in grace and understanding for a harsh father figure when you recognize that he struggles with work-related stress because of his unhealed wounds from his relationship with his father. Knowing that the origins and triggers of mental illness are beyond your control can help you accept it and move forward with treatment.

Discovering all the causes of mental illness is still a work in progress. But, in the last few years, we've made significant progress, and every new piece of knowledge we discover helps us strive toward more effective treatments and more stable and meaningful lives.

You cannot wholly chalk down mental illness or issues to your genes. It is crucial to remain informed about all risk and protective factors that can help you navigate this stressful diagnostic journey. Mental illness is not a generational "curse," no matter how unfortunate it may be. Many people live happy enough lives despite suffering from some disorder. However, we recommend you get a complete check-up of your family's history of mental illness. It can only help you in the long run.

That said, there is a crucial point to make about how to react when somebody in your family suffers from a mental health illness. One of the most compelling features of co-dependency, unhealthy attachment styles, and abandonment issues is the uncontrollable need to fix all the broken people in your life. If your early childhood had a significant caregiver who suffered from a mental health disorder, you would more likely reconstruct that dynamic in your adult life. Perhaps you believe that this time it will be different. This time you can heal them. This time they will see you and hear you and validate your existence. But the quest is doomed to fail. We don't have the power to save those around us. We can only keep ourselves.

It is possible to offer help, resources, compassion, and unconditional love to those who are dysregulated mentally or emotionally; however, it is ultimately up to them to seek help, stick to medication regimens, and build the support to help them heal.

Unfortunately, all too often, the sickest don't believe they are ill or need help. Some mental health conditions respond more favourably to treatment than others. People with narcissistic personality disorder, anti-social personality disorder (sociopaths), and psychopaths are reported to have minor success in mitigating their disturbance.

In fact, all will agree that these personality disorders cannot be treated or cured. At best, they learn to modify behaviours to "act" like they have improved when they have not. They only learned another skill; to "appear" healthy. One of the hallmark qualities of Cluster B disorders (including dramatic, overly emotional, or unpredictable thinking or behaviour) is the denial that they can be less than perfect. Their false selves are deluded and exist in an alternate reality far from the world the rest of us are consigned to. And people with schizoid disorders and other psychotic disorders also lack the agency to seek help or follow through with treatment plans because of their delusions and denial, not to mention paranoia and emotional paralysis.

As we have seen throughout this discussion, some will still argue that mental illness is a demonic possession. The history of treating the mentally ill and the origins of these illnesses are rife with misguided beliefs that led to cruelty and torture beyond the imagination.

When atrocities were not committed against the mentally ill, they were cast into "insane asylums" to languish and quietly wither away from the public eye. Mental illness was stigmatized and shamed into the shadows. There was no safe place for the dysregulated to live among "normal" society members.

With time and technology, new understandings of the etymology of brain disorders have come to light. But while progress has taken the folktales and superstitions out of the illness, misunderstanding prevails, and despite advocacy from many groups, it is still stigmatized. It's no wonder that families don't broadcast these diagnoses but attempt to manage them quietly behind closed doors.

People with mental health or addiction problems

are not always willing to seek treatment. They may not believe there is a problem. Or they may feel that they can address the issue independently, without treatment or intervention. You may be tempted to beg or threaten your family member to seek treatment repeatedly. Unfortunately, this often leads to a communication breakdown and the person shutting you out. You can try to find the right person who might approach them and have them suggest that the person see their family doctor or make an appointment for a mental health assessment.

All of this is tricky, indeed. More times than not, they will refuse treatment. If their safety or the safety of others in the home is at risk, it may be time for a 911 call that is undoubtedly hard to make.

When authorities are called in, there is always the possibility it will not be handled in a way that will resolve the issue and end up exacerbating the problem. If all else fails, there are legal avenues to have someone picked up and taken to a treatment facility for a 72-hour hold for evaluation and possibly long-term commitment if they threaten themselves or others.

When you can understand the dynamics of the brain and how it is made up, it will help to understand mental health and mental disorders. The entire concept of this book is to explain the neuroscience behind emotional wounds and how to prevent more damage to the emotional mind.

# REFERENCES

Lebow, H. I. (2021, July 2). *How does PTSD affect the brain? The physical effects of trauma.* Psych Central. Retrieved March 27, 2023, from https://psychcentral.com/ptsd/the-science-behind-ptsd-symptoms-how-trauma-changes-the-brain?slot_pos=article_1&utm_source=Sailthru+Email&utm_medium=Email&utm_campaign=weekly&utm_content=2023-01-25&apid=&rvid=a61d340305c0c28b12afbde3d63c30d3d9ae4dc9399ad609dd609e81b5119a9e combat-related PTSD. sciencedirect.com/science/article/pii/S2213158218301190

www.ingramcontent.com/pod-product-compliance
Lightning Source LLC
Chambersburg PA
CBHW010248010526
44119CB00054B/770